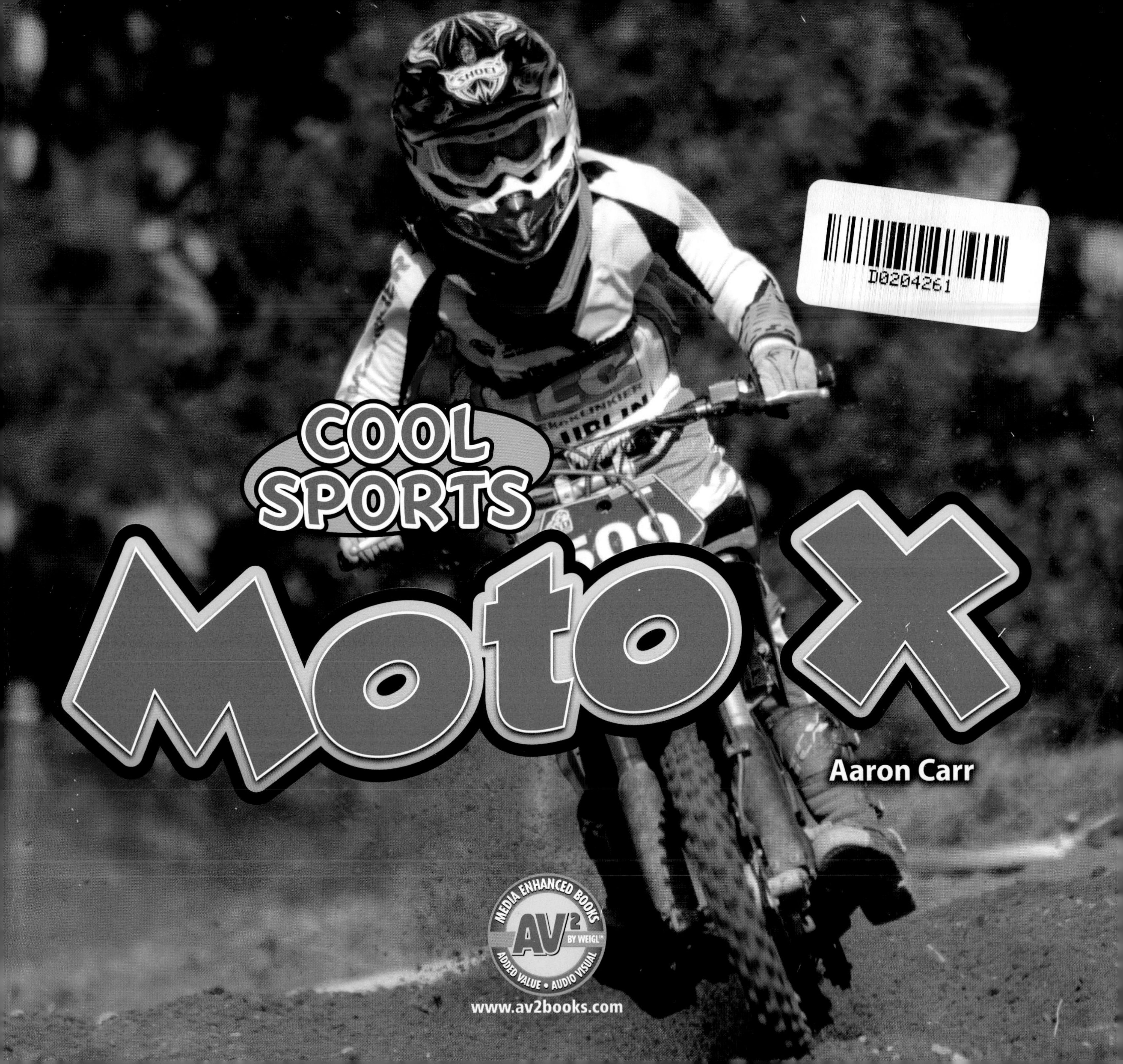

Cool Sports

Moto X

Aaron Carr

Media Enhanced Books
AV2 by Weigl™
Added Value • Audio Visual
www.av2books.com

Go to **www.av2books.com**, and enter this book's unique code.

BOOK CODE

P576957

AV² by Weigl brings you media enhanced books that support active learning.

AV² provides enriched content that supplements and complements this book. Weigl's AV² books strive to create inspired learning and engage young minds in a total learning experience.

Your AV² Media Enhanced books come alive with...

Audio
Listen to sections of the book read aloud.

Video
Watch informative video clips.

Embedded Weblinks
Gain additional information for research.

Try This!
Complete activities and hands-on experiments.

Key Words
Study vocabulary, and complete a matching word activity.

Quizzes
Test your knowledge.

Slide Show
View images and captions, and prepare a presentation.

... and much, much more!

Published by AV² by Weigl
350 5th Avenue, 59th Floor, New York, NY 10118
Website: www.av2books.com www.weigl.com

Library of Congress Cataloguing in Publication data available upon request.
Fax 1-866-449-3445 for the attention of the Publishing Records department.

ISBN 978-1-61913-511-6 (hard cover)
ISBN 978-1-61913-517-8 (soft cover)

Printed in the United States of America in North Mankato, Minnesota
4 5 6 7 8 9 17 16 15 14 13

072013
WEP110613

Editor: Aaron Carr Art Director: Terry Paulhus
Weigl acknowledges Getty Images as the primary image supplier for this title.

COOL SPORTS

Moto X

CONTENTS

ACERBIS
25

Moto X is a sport.
People ride motorbikes over jumps and along a track.

Moto X bikes are small and light. They are made for going over jumps and racing on dirt tracks.

Like a PRO

Pro moto X riders do tricks on their bikes.

Moto X riders should always wear a helmet. Helmets keep riders safe when they fall.

Like a PRO

Pro moto X riders wear moto X suits to keep them safe.

People ride moto X bikes on dirt tracks. These tracks can be in the woods or in a place made for moto X.

Like a PRO

Pro moto X riders drive on tracks with big ramps.

Practice is very important. Riders must practice often to become good at moto X.

Like a PRO

Pro moto X riders practice for many hours each day.

Moto X riders jump off a ramp and do a trick. This is called Best Trick.

Like a PRO

Pro moto X riders jump high in the air to do tricks.

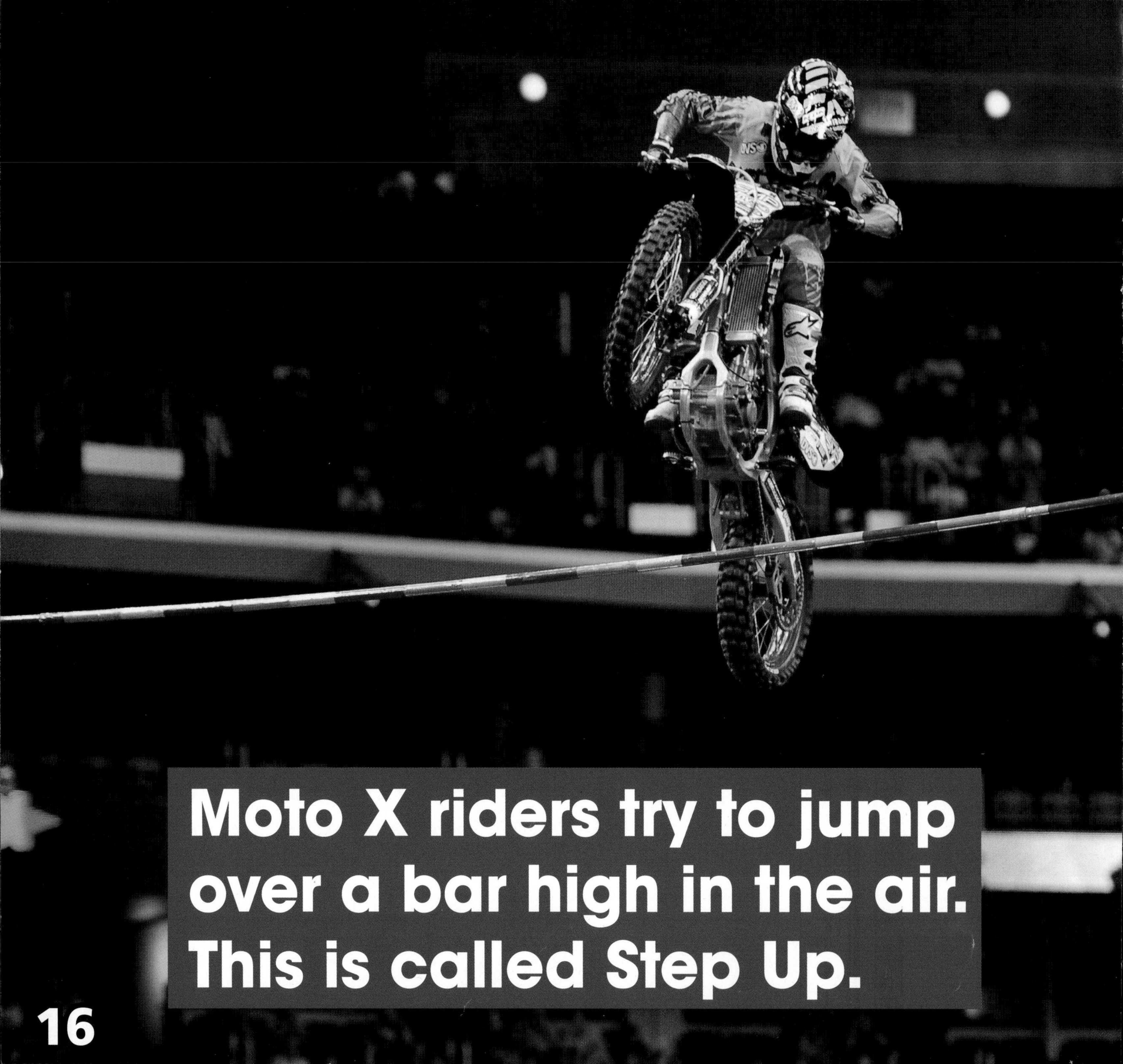

Moto X riders try to jump over a bar high in the air. This is called Step Up.

Like a PRO

Pro moto X riders try to jump as high as they can.

Moto X riders race around a course with three kinds of track. This is called Supermoto.

Like a PRO

Moto X riders drive fast to finish the race first.

MICHELIN
MOTUL
DC
SHOWA
CERNICS
RK
MCR
TAG

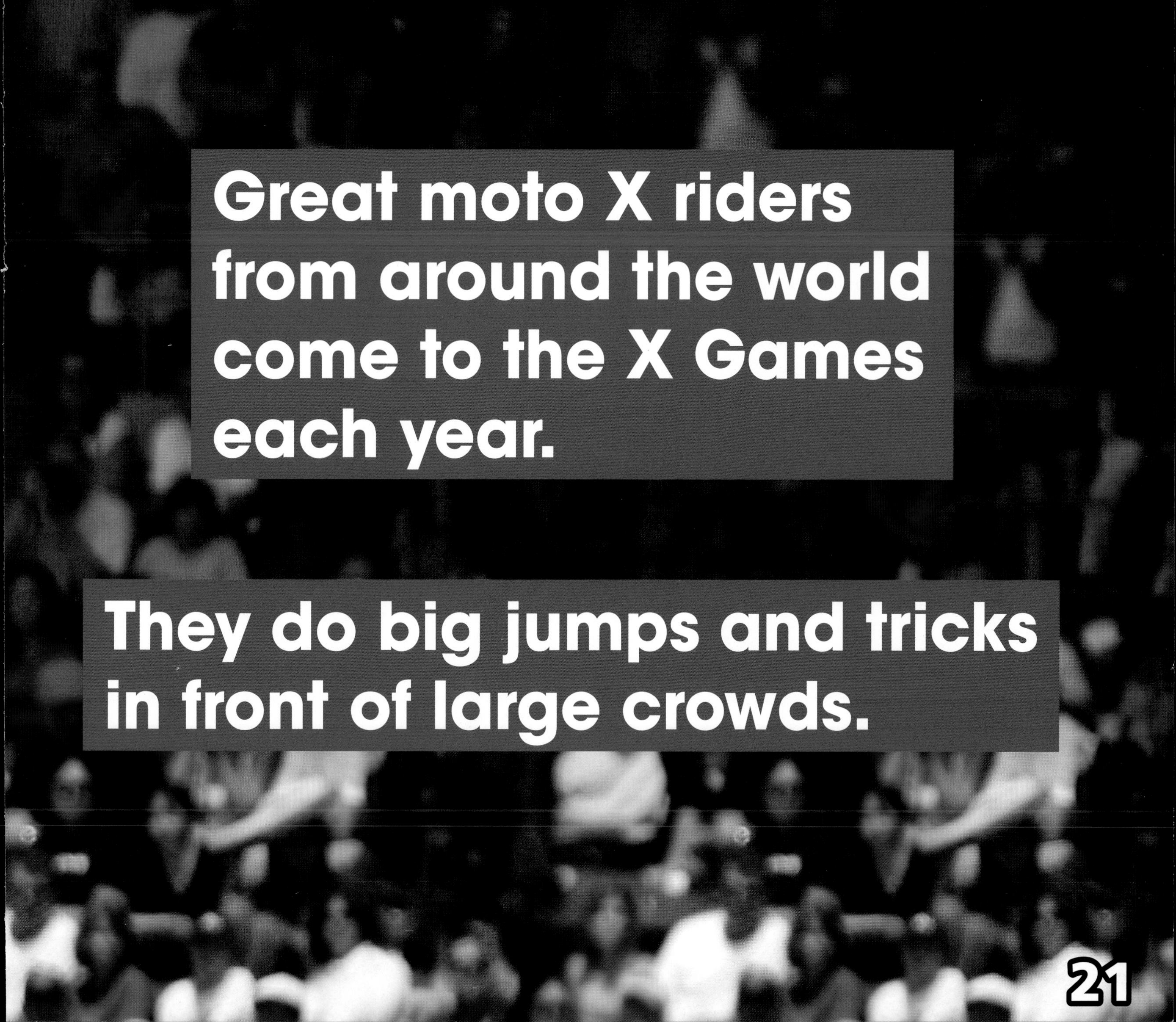

Great moto X riders from around the world come to the X Games each year.

They do big jumps and tricks in front of large crowds.

MOTO X FACTS

These pages provide detailed information that expands on the interesting facts found in this book. These pages are intended to be used by adults as a learning support to help young readers round out their knowledge of each sport in the *Cool Sports* series.

Pages 4–5

Moto X, or motocross, is a sport that requires skill, determination, and balance. Riders use specially designed motorcycles to race around dirt tracks and over obstacles. Sometimes, riders perform tricks such as flips and jumps. Moto X is based on a British off-road sport called scrambles, which began in 1924.

Pages 6–7

Moto X bikes are designed to be lightweight and very durable. They must be able to withstand the extreme forces caused by landing high jumps. These bikes are smaller than normal motorcycles and have smaller, louder engines. In order to keep their weight down, moto X bikes do not have speedometers, lights, or even kickstands. The seat is long and flat to allow riders to change position during tricks.

Pages 8–9

The helmet is the most important piece of safety equipment. When falling off a motorcycle, the rider's head may hit the ground. Helmets have saved many riders from serious head injuries. Moto X riders also wear moto X suits, padded gloves and boots, and chest protectors to keep them safe. Their helmets feature a full face shield and goggles to protect the face and eyes.

Pages 10–11

Freestyle moto X can be done anywhere there is plenty of open space and dirt. Natural tracks can be found on public land and may have dirt and rock ramps, hills, and jumps. Some riders build their own tracks. Pro moto X tracks are built for safety and to allow riders to reach great heights for tricks. The tracks include ramps with landing areas, dirt piled into hills and bumps, and padded bumpers for safety.

Pages 12–13

Practice is the most important part of becoming good at any sport. Most professional moto X riders practice for many hours every day. They push themselves to improve their skills by trying new tricks and riding styles. Some moto X riders try to invent new tricks. They must practice these tricks many times to ensure they can repeat the moves properly in competitions.

Pages 14–15

Best Trick is one of the most extreme moto X competitions. Ten riders each take two jumps off a dirt-covered ramp. After launching off the ramp, riders perform tricks in the air and land on another dirt ramp that helps them slow down. Tricks include backflips, front flips, and corkscrews. Riders are judged on style and the difficulty of the trick.

Pages 16–17

The Step Up competition is a high jump event for moto X riders. Two vertical bars are set on top of a wall of dirt. A horizontal bar is then laid between the two bars at a height of 26 to 29 feet (8 to 9 meters). Riders take turns riding off a ramp to jump over the bar. If they cannot clear the bar, they are eliminated. The bar is raised 6 inches (15 centimeters) each round. The event continues until only one rider is left.

Pages 18–19

Supermoto is a combination of moto X and road racing. Supermoto courses feature three types of track—flat dirt track, moto X style dirt track with jumps and bumps, and smooth pavement. The layout of the track changes often, and it is filled with obstacles throughout. Riders must navigate dirt and steel jumps, high-speed straightaways, and twisting corners on their way to the finish line.

Pages 20–21

The Summer X Games is an annual sports tournament that showcases the best athletes in the extreme sports world. The X Games started in 1995. The competition includes events for moto X, skateboarding, BMX, and rallycross. The X Games attract the best extreme athletes from around the world each year. Some events feature athletes flying 40 feet (12 m) above the ground.

KEY WORDS

Research has shown that as much as 65 percent of all written material published in English is made up of 300 words. These 300 words cannot be taught using pictures or learned by sounding them out. They must be recognized by sight. This book contains 56 common sight words to help young readers improve their reading fluency and comprehension. This book also teaches young readers several important content words. These words are paired with pictures to aid in learning and improve understanding.

Page	Sight Words First Appearance
5	a, along, and, is, people, over
6	are, for, light, made, on, small, they
7	do, like, their
8	always, keep, should, when
9	them, to
10	be, can, in, or, place, the, these
11	big, with
12	at, good, important, must, often, very
13	day, each, many
14	off, this
15	air, high
16	try
17	as
18	around, kinds, of, three
19	first
21	come, from, great, world, year

Page	Content Words First Appearance
5	jumps, motorbikes, moto X, sport, track
6	bikes
7	pro, riders, tricks
8	helmet
9	suits
10	woods
11	ramps
12	practice
13	hours
14	Best Trick
16	bar, Step Up
18	course, Supermoto
19	race
21	crowds, X Games

MEDIA ENHANCED BOOKS AV² BY WEIGL ADDED VALUE • AUDIO VISUAL

Check out www.av2books.com for activities, videos, audio clips, and more!

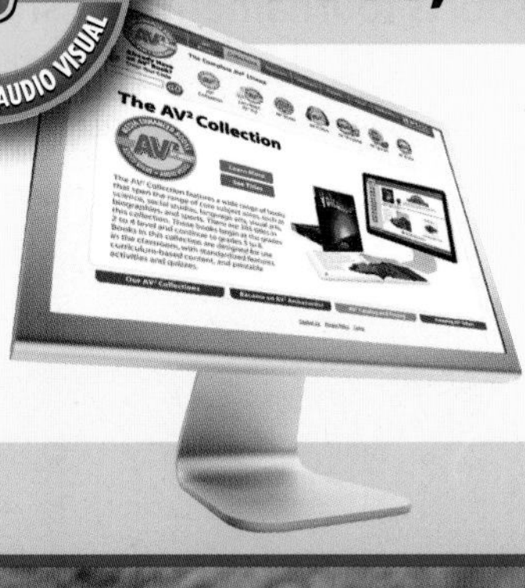

1. **Go to www.av2books.com.**
2. **Enter book code.** P576957
3. **Fuel your imagination online!**

www.av2books.com